POETRY IS DANGEROUS,
THE POET IS AN OUTLAW

OTHER BOOKS BY TONY MOFFEIT:

Neon Peppers. Cherry Valley, New York: Cherry Valley Editions, 1992.

Luminous Animal. Cherry Valley, New York: Cherry Valley Editions, 1989.

Boogie Alley. Erie, Pennsylvania: Kangaroo Court Publishing, 1989.

Pueblo Blues. Cherry Valley, New York: Cherry Valley Editions, 1986.

POETRY VIDEOS FEATURING TONY MOFFEIT:

Mad Man Junkyard Blues. Thornton, Colorado: Stone River Productions, 1990.

Outlaw. Thornton, Colorado: Stone River Productions, 1990.

Poetry Is Dangerous:
The Poet Is An Outlaw

Tony Moffeit

A Great Basin Book
FLOATING ISLAND PUBLICATIONS
CEDARVILLE
1995

ISBN: 0-912449-44-6

Published by:

Floating Island Publications
P.O. Box 341
Cedarville, California 96104

Some of the poems in this volume have previously appeared in:
*Atom Mind, The Taos Review, Desperado, The Chiron Review, Abbey,
Amelia, The Charlotte Poetry Review, The Current, Ghost Moon Over
Pueblo, The Bloomsbury Review, Caprice, Cokefish, Rosebud Forum,
Six Guns* and *The Eleventh Muse.*

The essay, "Dancing With the Ghosts of the Dead," previously
appeared in *Tracks In The Snow: Essays By Colorado Poets*, Ray
Gonzalez, ed. Arvada, Colorado: Mesilla Press Publishing, 1989.

This first edition of one thousand copies numbered and signed
by the author.

For information regarding an audiotape of Tony Moffeit
performing portions of this book, write: The Pueblo Poetry
Project, 1501 E. 7th, Pueblo, Colorado 81001.

for Miles

CONTENTS

Run with Stray Dogs in the Tambourine Dust

11 :: run with stray dogs in the tambourine dust

Dreaming of Crazy Horse

19 :: dreaming of crazy horse
21 :: buffalo dance
22 :: tomahawk sundown
23 :: always the dark rain
24 :: dancing alone
25 :: crickets and mosquitoes
26 :: to be born again
27 :: phantom canyon dancer
28 :: dancing with the ghosts of the dead

Keep A Knockin But You Can't Come In

33 :: drifter of dark dreams
34 :: voodoo snake woman blues
35 :: mad man junkyard blues
36 :: sing me one more time that ramblin fever
37 :: indian summer
38 :: keep a knockin but you can't come in
40 :: one night
42 :: juggling starfish
44 :: blood of the poet/the death of lorca
45 :: poetry is dangerous, the poet is an outlaw

Outlaw Blues

49 :: outlaw
50 :: the night singing in her nerves
51 :: blood moon
52 :: marguerita
53 :: black silk
54 :: demon sway
55 :: red weather
56 :: the itch
58 :: blue haze of dream of demon sway

Ghost Dancer

63 :: high range
64 :: ojo caliente
66 :: under my fingers
67 :: ghost dancer
68 :: didn't even know what day it was
69 :: giving birth to thunder
70 :: lightning in slow motion

Poetry Is Dangerous, The Poet Is An Outlaw:
Essays on Poetry and the Art of the Individual

75 :: Dancing with the Ghosts of the Dead
78 :: The Outlaw Spirit in American Culture
83 :: A Revolution of the Individual
89 :: Poetry and the Art of the Individual
94 :: The Secret Language of the Individual

RUN WITH STRAY DOGS IN THE TAMBOURINE DUST

run with stray dogs in the tambourine dust

she was the queen of the cantina blues
a dream that danced like voodoo fire
and i was a drifter a coyote lurking
around the ramshackle wood of the chickencoop
the night was one of no stars no moon
a name is breath and breath is wind
and wind is the movement of a woman
brushing against your chest making the
hair stand up on the back of your neck
i think i have been in this town too long
i need to ride a mystery train
hear that long snake moan
run with stray dogs in the tambourine dust
where the strippers aren't nearly nasty enough
and the bullet itch of billy the kid
dances all night in the back of my head

i have burnt myself out so i can sing again
for the dead cannot dance cannot cry in the wind
i want to go back to bayou st. john
congo square lake pontchartrain
feel the gris gris in the mambo air
visit the grave of one called marie marie marie
when i am old and all is said and done
i'll be a voodoo king on bourbon street
the conjure man with secret eyes secret hands
his mojo is invisible they'll say
he is a dancing ghost in a vanishing wind

or maybe a medicine man in taos square
with the adobe pulsing from the beat of my drum
while a woman dances with a long black snake
her body twisting to the whip of the serpent
writhing her sagebrush blues
and i'll be singing a song you can't understand

talking in tongues
slurring my syllables because of my blood
the nerve the pulse the beating of the drum within

i want turtle give me turtle
i want crow give me crow
i want buzzard give me buzzard
back in oklahoma the earth is red
the red earth the blue sky the green trees
and the leaves blowing laughing
my mother just a girl
when she gave birth to me
a child giving birth to a child
then she died young
and it's all in my veins the ghost dance
of living and dying
of laughing and crying
dancing along the river's edge
the convulsive moon
of the cherokees

the sun i know the sun
the sun breaking through a turquoise rain
as i stroke the throat of my lover
i want to go back
to skull and bone and dust and stone
the face of my father before i was born
the prairie wolf the desert rat the cactus wren
the burrowing owl the jackrabbit
footprints of the shadowdance
and now i feel the warm pulse of green chile
in a neighborhood bar
a woman with skin of avocados
the mountains in the distance
clouds of shadows

as careful as coyote i move
for to be free is to be untrusting
today i do not shave
i sleep in
the sun throws circles through the curtains
as if my bedroom were a plaza
and outside cordova walks by
cursing at the top of his lungs
about nothing
his curses are a song
a madman's rhythms
a blues for the east side

on my wall hangs a hat decorated with feathers
the hat of the chicken king
beneath it a washboard
one day i will attach bells to it
and play it with thimbles on the streets of new orleans
next to the washboard are black boots of brushed leather
with spurs that jingle jangle like tambourines
little death bells
for the mysteries of the street

to identify the legends in the flesh
the dance of the mirror of the dream
i want to go back to the swamp
the wetness that is woman
the darkness that is night
and hear the sharp cries of voodoo ceremonials
bodies that must be naked
to be purified by mud
i want to croak my blues like a bullfrog
shake like an alligator
writhe like a diamondback
be possessed by the spirit power
i am one with the swamp rose

i am one with the night heron
i am one with the hanging cypress
i am one with the cottonmouth
i am one with the locusts
i am one with the voodoo drum

or christmas day at taos pueblo
the clowns shouting laughing playing tricks
and the tribal dancers with dirty fists
cutting the sacred meat of the antelope
and i go back to crazy horse geronimo
walk in dusty boots by indian graves
do a dance of my own in the middle of my chest
feel the hair of an indian maiden
like strands of chile peppers brushing my neck
pocahontas sacajawea hear my cry
i wrench from my guts a desert blues
hear it in the caw of a crow
on the wire of a fence
hear it in the howl of the
prairie wolf hiding beneath sagebrush
hear it in the chants of the deer dance

i want to dance a wild dance of lonesome wolves
i want to stalk a path out in the wilderness
then come down from the mesa
like the ancient ones
with nothing in their hands
empty-handed i come to you
no gifts nothing but my nakedness
and a hunger for the cliffs
reach me in my agony
my madness is your mystery
the secret heartbeat
that comes back to touch the people

i was born in the land of the red man
the son of the mad man the used car dealer
the trickster with the mad laugh
the land of the diamondback
the junkyard the traintracks
cottonwood cottonmouth ramshackle dance
the endless laugh of the mad man
where clouds float like smoke signals
or spirits of the dead
and the bones have long forgotten
the scar tissue

and now i sing with my blood
of a woman named marguerita
and her sensual healing
how love is a struggle
hard as iron as fragile
as a dream a bubble
and how i work the muscles
in her back and shoulders and neck
says she feels the energy
from my hands my fingers
how it is all a dance

DREAMING OF CRAZY HORSE

dreaming of crazy horse

you dreamed of my death,
ghost sister, then i spun
on black ice and rolled
my car over the cliff
dreaming of crazy horse
dreaming of a talking drum
there was a passionate
whine in the wind like
a baby's cry, was that you,
ghost sister, or just
some spanish witch along
the borderline as i felt
like tumbling dice a
trapeze act a somersault
in the sky you dreamed of
my death then i rode the
curve the fall dreaming of
crazy horse dreaming of
a talking drum and that
gnawing deep in the guts
to go beyond to leave
behind your shadow to find
the fire to lick the blaze
to drink the flames
i looked in the rearview
mirror and saw blood on
my face smeared like
warpaint a magic wound
a beautiful nightmare
you dreamed of my death

then i floated in a
timeless moment dreaming
of a talking drum a
mask a skull a tooth
a bone now i walk in
dust the powder of stone
the glass of black ice
dreaming of a dancing
ghost the black snow
against the white sky

buffalo dance

the slope of your back
ceremonial grounds
marguerita the muscles
of your back the
skin of drums your
profile a kachina
mask every movement
a buffalo dance
i hear crow and
coyote in your groans
the sun lifts the
rain of your forehead
your breasts a mirage
for my thirst
we stomp in circles
awaiting the sacred
meat the spirits
of the dead

tomahawk sundown

speak to me
you ghosts you phantoms
i hunger for your breath
speak to me
in daredevil skies
smeared with blood
stained with ink
i want to feel
the buffalo dance
in your trail of dust
speak to me
you ghosts you phantoms
my eyes are open
my hands are empty
i want to drink
your vision
embrace your passion
speak to me
in skulls and bones
in tomahawk shadows
speak to me
you ghosts you phantoms

always the dark rain

always the dark rain
marguerita always this
dark arrowed rain
we are always dancers
in the dark rain as
your shadow becomes
my shadow your eyes
darts in the dark rain
the train whistle's
whine and your body
of black lightning
in the dark rain
always your cobra
thighs marguerita
and your barroom scars
in the black rain
always the dark rain
and we are dancers
in shattered mirrors
in veins of dream
leaking black rain

dancing alone

i seek zebra and cobra
and mother-of-pearl
i seek outlaw twilight
of yucca plazas
i seek egypt in your eyes
the strange winds
along the borderline
tell me a secret
that makes truth a lie
speak to me of silence
i want abandoned rooms
abandoned places
old filling stations
ancient motels of moss
and rain adobe hideouts
coyote hollows where
one can dance alone
feel the roaring
silence of red weather
yet you are never alone
for the ghosts always
find you voices echoing
in the night wind
voices howling with
wild abandon voices
surrendering to the
darkness the nerves
take it all the edge
of the wound the
trace of the scar
the phantom breath
that renews the ache
of that ecstasy the
rhythm caught in the
heart of the blues

crickets and mosquitoes

crickets and mosquitoes
marguerita crickets and
mosquitoes in the fields
while a taos moon rolls
green across the sky
and the rambler the
gambler risks a river
and pulls the ace from
his sleeve crickets and
mosquitoes marguerita
and spanish guitars
in no name adobe bars
crickets and mosquitoes
in your gypsy blood
your jungle scars in
the circle of your arms
your smell of earth
crickets and mosquitoes
and windchimes ringing in
your veins pulse rhythm
rolling for the lightning
shooting up your spine

to be born again

i beat the drum
i pound the drum
the earthdrum
the womandrum
the howling drum
of ghost dance
to be born again
the sky calling
cloudfoam calling
turning changing
grass shooting
to be born again
the word bleeding
to be born again
i beat the drum
i pound the drum
to be born again
and again and again

phantom canyon dancer

out of the fullness
of empty space i learn
to drink your silence
you take the ore from
the mines the diamonds
from the skyline so i
can hear you say things
that have no words
it's your ghost i want
not your flesh not your
mind not even your soul
just your ghost i
found in the deepest
vein of your passion
a part of me that's
invisible a phantom
sometimes i think i
catch your image in
my mirror if you dream
i am dead i will come
alive if you dream i
am alive i will haunt
you with my darkness
i want the deepest
part of you it's
your ghost i want

dancing with the ghosts of the dead

a hunger a passion for invisibility
an obsession to dance in phantom canyon
to knife the sky in ecstasy
to emerge from a forest and stand
on the edge of a cliff a thirst for
poison black bridges tree shadows
a thirst for ghosts for soil for sand
i want blue corn and turquoise and silver
i want indian graves and underground rivers
i want the earth to speak to me
in the body of a woman i want
drums and masks and throbbing
cannibal rhythms i want the intensity
of taking the essence of the moment
i want to drink some laughter
i want to eat some agony
i want to burn with a vision
i want crazy horse in my head
i want to sing with fire
a blaze that erupts in the blood
i want to speak in ancient tongues
animal syllables cobra rhythms
i want to dance with the bones
i want to dream a rambling gambling fever
reach me in my hunger
tonight i want to leave

KEEP A KNOCKIN BUT YOU CAN'T COME IN

drifter of dark dreams

'when people start talkin
bout goin somewhere'
he said 'i'm the kind of
guy who has already got
up and went'

and that was woody guthrie
and nobody knew him but
the people nobody knew him
but the boxcar hobo and
the dust bowl refugee

he was walt whitman and
billy the kid and manolete
he had leadbelly's blues
and lorca's duende and
you could hear the pain
in that rusty dusty voice

i once visited his house
in okemah torn down
except for walls filled
with scribblings:
'it's not that we ever
knew you nor know you now,
but we shore can appreciate
where you've come from'

voodoo snake woman blues

the voodoo woman says it's easy
talking about the way she moves
it's easy easy so doggone easy
all you gotta do is feel the blues
dressed in black in the casa del
where everyone stands still
when she dances where everyone
stops breathing when she slinks
and slides to a lowdown blues
independence is free to breathe
is to dance is to feel the
obsessive beat she says
talking about the way she moves
on the dancefloor or on the way
to the bar to order a whiskey
sour everyone waiting for her
to enter the dancefloor again
her eyes hypnotic her black
dress cobra tight and the night
is nothing more than her
twisting and sliding the
night is nothing more than her
disappearance into the breath
into the blues into the
obsessive beat her identity
is waiting her identity is
waiting her identity is
waiting in the blackness of
the mirror in the blackness
of the glass in the blackness
of the dance

mad man junkyard blues

i sang the blues in my father's junkyard
salvage yard boneyard of old cars rusted-
out autos broken-down jalopies smashed-up
glass banged-up metal down there by the
train tracks in claremore, oklahoma
i sang the blues in the mad man's salvage
mad to shout mad to joke mad to dance
mad to yell mad to laugh mad to live
i wrote my first poems in the torn-up
automobiles among the dust and weeds
under the dark moon of an oklahoma sky
waiting for saturday night poker games
in our bachelor shack on the hill where
all the mechanics would show up to toss
dollar bills on a scratched-up coffee
table sweating and betting while the
wind blew wild and the mad man told
his jokes and laughed his laugh an
endless mad rolling shaking laugh that
swept away everything in its path
i sang the blues in the mad man's
junkyard to the sound of the train
whistle and the howls of hobos and
the flashing of lightning bugs and
a ghost wind through the cottonwoods

sing me one more time that ramblin fever

i hear the train whistle in the night
and think of all those miles of
mississippi delta backroads where
robert johnson rambled with nothing
more than his guitar his voice
his songs and even now through
the scratchy grooves feel
the rich earth of his words

i hear the train whistle in the night
and see a scarecrow at the crossroads
where robert johnson rambled stalking
a dog from hell searching for a
cracked mirror in the bathroom
of a roadhouse shadowing the
figure of a voodoo woman in
the lightning of his slide

i hear the train whistle in the night
and see the dirty kitchens where
robert johnson rambled his blues
his moan bringing the rain like a
ghost dancer a dust devil a
wind of wolves there in the
shadows shoulders hunched from
behind fretting low for the light

indian summer

cordova sits on
his front porch
writing until
dusk when he wraps
himself in an
indian blanket
like a witch doctor
and dissolves in
the pueblo night
i drive by night
after night and
he never moves
staring straight
ahead transfixed
like a witch doctor
in a navajo trance
except tonight
when he leaps
from his chair
and dances on
his lawn tearing
what he has written
into little shreds
of paper and
throwing them into
the air and they
fall like snow
on his dancing
shoulders his
front lawn like
frost in the
blue haze of
indian summer

keep a knockin but you can't come in

the silent rhinocerous walks alone
never fearing what others think of him
while i twist in midnight saloons
trying to walk through the silver mirror
voodoo women make my bed under a mojo moon
if you are looking for a miracle
raise your hand if you are looking
for a miracle close your eyes
soak in the invisible rhythm of the void
i hear the last words of my mother
before her death telling me about
the first time i laughed a baby on a
blanket under a tree the leaves
dancing and swishing and i couldn't
stop laughing it was one of the finest
moments of her life she said and now
i want to know dance the laughing dance
the dancing laughter drunk on the
rhythm of the shaking leaves
tonight the moon is playing with the
stormclouds dodging and weaving
striped by the blackness stained
by the blackness and the roadhouse
is jumping with the refrain
keep a knockin but you can't come in
keep a knockin but you can't come in

and a voodoo woman wants to dance
and when she moves everyone stands
still everyone stops breathing
i only realized how my mother and i
were connected after her death
that umbilical cord of the soul
that was never cut it taught me that
we are all ghosts connecting with
other ghosts in some invisible manner
because in some way she is much more
alive now speaks to me in a dancing
laugh a laughing dance of leaves

one night

a lonely horn blowing through the night
like a fire
roaring like a train whistle
like a fire
a lonely horn blowing through the smoke
like a fire
and the night comes alive
and the dark becomes light
a lonely woman moves with the blues
and the wolves howl
down by the tracks
a lonely woman moves with the blues
and the snakes slide
in the shadows
the willows move outside the window
the willows move in the rain
a lonely woman moves with the blues
a lonely horn blows through the night
like a fire
like a train whistle
like a rain whistle
like a wolf howling
down by the tracks
like a snake sliding
in the shadows

no place to hide but the night
no place to run but the darkness
no place to hide but the night
no rain to drink but the darkness
no place to hide but the night
no dice to roll but the darkness
no place to hide but the night
a train whistle blows through the darkness
like a jazz horn
a train whistle blows through the darkness
like a ghost horn
a train whistle blows through the darkness
like a blues horn
a woman dances alone in the darkness
through a desert
through the space of waiting
a woman dances alone in the darkness
through the ecstasy of her wounds
through a train whistle
through a jazz horn
through a blues horn
through a ghost moan
through a dream song
a woman dances alone in the darkness
invisible

juggling starfish

she climbs the railing
of the bridge and looks
down at dark fish at
quicksilver in which
she wishes to dive
at a river of stars
the eye of the jaguar
her hands gripping iron
she is cliff diver
cloud crier wanting
to twist into water
feel the cool alcohol
of the creek the moss
of stones the galaxies
of the lovebed her
nostrils filled with
afterrain afterbirth
the prospector's dig
the archaeology of her
fear she bites her fist
and looks into a black
mirror and sees only
shadow bright moments
that are drowned
no light in this
night alone the breeze
licking her feet

the dust whirling
like a lover while
she is on a highwire
without a net a
tightrope walker
juggling starfish
she dreams she cannot
touch the ground
her eyes roll into
the back of the sky
arms open for the
rain to drink the
wind to breathe

blood of the poet/the death of lorca

i have nothing to say
about your death, federico
about your body thrown into a grave
dug by yourself
i have nothing to say
about your being placed against a wall
and guns raised to shoulders
with barrels like the eyes
of the bull meeting yours
i cannot speak
about the fire that would breathe down
to snatch away bones and flesh and soul
i cannot speak
of frogs and crickets and toads
the birthwater the bullfighter
the arrow of song
i have nothing to say
about the guns with horns
metallic bulls
the earth you feared
would turn to machine
i have nothing to say
about no crowd to mourn
your blood in the sand
no fixed hour for the ritual passing
i cannot speak
about the blood of the poet
who lives alone who dies alone
yet is never alone
i cannot speak
of your dancing ghost
nor of the night wind
surrendering to the dawn

poetry is dangerous, the poet is an outlaw

poetry is dangerous, the poet is an outlaw
poetry is dangerous, the poet is an outlaw
walt whitman was dangerous
walt whitman was an outlaw
walt whitman said take to the open road
walt whitman was an outlaw
walt whitman said he who touches my words
touches flesh and blood
poetry is dangerous, the poet is an outlaw
woody guthrie was dangerous
woody guthrie was an outlaw
woody guthrie took to the open road
with a voice that gave us a hard word
a word that no prison can hold
a word that no chain can drag down
a word that no weapon can defeat
that hard word
liberty
poetry is dangerous, the poet is an outlaw
garcia lorca was dangerous
garcia lorca was an outlaw
they dragged him out of his house
put him up against a wall
and shot him
not because he was a politician
not because he was a criminal
but because he was a poet
they can kill the poet
but they cannot kill the word
they can kill the poet
but they cannot kill the spirit
they can kill the poet
but they cannot kill the people

OUTLAW BLUES

outlaw

the night is alive with a thousand eyes
let the outlaw enter the streets
and all becomes gunfire foreplay
the risks too high for the stakes
the roulette wheel spinning for the snake
poker-dealing saxophone women
stripping to the cards
how many notches on his gunbelt?
how many tattoos on her legs?

the night is alive with a thousand eyes
let the outlaw dance with the danger he meets
and all becomes lightning poison
the blues of the edges
words that are bullets that rip the flesh
words that are knives that flash in the darkness
killers of cages and chains

the night singing in her nerves

coyotes drank the shadows
while she moved
that was her secret
all she had to do
was feel the blues

she sought the outlaw
on nights when the
moon howled and a
drumbeat pulsed
in her veins

she sat in the corner
booth in the back
of the saloon in the
wildness of her silence
in the ghost dance
of her disappearance

the leaves shook
outside the window
the darkness became
her blood the roadhouse
jumped with her rhythm

coyotes drank the shadows
while she moved
that was her secret
all she had to do
was feel the blues

blood moon

i live like
a cobra
holed up
in the night
or a boa
reflected
in the mirror
of your face
when nothing
is left but
our cannibal
mouths and
a saxophone
that rips
the blues
from the guts
anonymous
fingers that
heal the
darkness
alleyway
backstairs
where beat
the lowdown
hearts of
hobos looking
for bottles
with a last
drop of
thunderbird
or lovers
in old hotels
chasing the
ghosts of
buffalo

marguerita

balancing on
a high wire
like a gun
fighter

your eyes
as wild as
roadside
flowers

dreamed a
grave an
open mouth
a cave

the crazy
fire of
your lips
alive

black silk

devil river moans
like the blues
in my bones

i want to ride home
on your skin of
magnolia

i want to rip away
the mirror of your
shadow find the
echo of your face

fire to taste
the tongue the rain
to drink the blaze

in the streets
at night i listen
for your name

demon sway

it's like
walking in
a waking
dream
stalking
your shadow
woman
your
secrets
revealed
in a blues
moan the
yellow
lights of
mill bars
rain nights
wind blade
cutting
like
tequila
& i'm lost
in the
salt & the
chatter
of barmaids
your name
leaking
down the
windows

red weather

when coyote
  howls
    his
old-time blues
  i feel
    your
wolf-nature
  breaking loose
    remember
mountain sky
  the curve
    of spine
the tongue
  of your eyes
    you
the ghost
  in the
  phone line
    the fire
of the
  jaguar
    to open
a jungle
  the clock
that itches
  your wetness
    a legend

the itch

twisted
that night
like a
misfit in
a ditch
risk
was more
than a
word
when i
looked
into your
gunpowder
eyes
& motor
cycles were
backfiring
in the
alley
passersby
skeletons &
shadows
w/knives in
their spines
& i didn't
have to
consult a
thesaurus
to find a
synonym
for danger

it was
your name
your arms
your legs
& that itch
you were
so good
at scratching

blue haze of dream of demon sway

i stalk the dark of the moon
for the rain that drinks me
a booth in a bar to move to
the black-eyed blues blue haze
of dream of demon sway a naked
moan from the street outside
i have nothing to say my body
does the talkin stalkin the
dream the nightmare the vision
see my eyes shift slowly to
the side as my shoulders
feel the rhythm i hear the moon
and know midnight is coming
smoke and shadow rain and dust
the skeletal kiss of the
dancefloor the naked torso of
midnight big dice tumbling
look at them snake eyes your
body trembling under my touch
i leave my fingerprints on
your spine you call my name
you ask who i am i am who i am
the one who dances with the
living and the dead as you
feel the beat in your back
in your neck under my x-ray
eyes you laugh like a river
as we dance alone together

solitary phantoms a blues in
the night a grunt a groan a
noise from the street the slick
asphalt reflecting neon the
blast of horns the pour of rain
the surging rhythm of the blues
remember me as the touch that
is left on your body the feel
that is left in your moves

GHOST DANCER

high range

we were lost that night
marguerita in the
brooding shadows of
the diablo mountains
lost in a daze lost in
a fever of our
separateness
yucca blades like
whips like knives
for the glance that
enters you like a blade
gunshots in the wind
the bark of a wolf
men impersonating gods
and it was only your
skin between madness
and escape turning
the dilemmas to dust
we were dancing spiders
in adobe shadows
from behind as if
your body pressed
against glass

ojo caliente

the journey begins
in taos, new mexico
blue mountain
and you travel southwest
you must go
it is your destiny
past an old bus
'special knowledge of
the divine mysteries'
painted on the side
you turn at the marker
that reads 'taos junction'
and you travel southwest
you must go
it is your destiny
you drive through
a canyon of phantoms
past the cactus rose
and ghost blossoms
and phantom birds
floating on air currents
rocks with cryptic messages:
lauri loves leroy
angel tom
you emerge on a
mountain top
and descend into a valley
and you travel southwest
you must go
it is your destiny

you come upon
a place called ojo caliente
magic water
hot baths
and an ancient porch
where you wrap yourself
in a serape
dreaming among the hollyhocks
staring into the sky
and then you dance

under my fingers

i stalked your shadow
through the streets
of santa fe weighing
the risks against the
stakes balancing an
old blues on the
saloon mirror while
the strobe licked
your throat and the
blackness spoke in
wizard tongues as
you moved like a
ghost on the balcony
later you whispered
through tears how
it was all worth it
said it never fails
this flame that
brings the rain

ghost dancer

your words annihilate everything
i want to sleep by the tracks
sort out the real and the unreal
come creeping along the horizon
like a ghost out of control
the phone lines are dangerous
don't remind me of those outlaw
nights your face in a flash of
lightning be careful when it rains
night storm the rattlesnake rain
i am the wind i am sending back
your spirit i am coming to you
in a dream skin peeled like old
wallpaper the scars traced by the
edge of a fingernail you just
drink dust like rain your brain
singing to break free i see your
face and your liquid movements
shedding your skin like a snake
just once understand the silence
the veins of the dream turning
returning and the only escape is
to do deeper into the heart of
the wound nothing is real the
streets leaking secrets of
letting go under a timeless sky
uncoiled loneness touching
loneness in the outlaw night
the dream of the mirror the
mirror of the dream arrows of
rain giving shape to the
shadows or the tongue of the
flame drinking the whispers
always driving looking for
something till there's nothing
left in the blood but the blaze

didn't even know what day it was

you always told me to
turn down the fire as
i fried bacon in my
t-shirt the hot grease
splattering on my arms
leaving little nicks
of burns but i didn't
care didn't even know
what day it was when
you roamed the house
in your robe and the
cat stretched out on
the window sill as
i ate eggs and grits
and fried green
tomatoes before going
back to bed and i
never did learn to
turn down the fire

giving birth to thunder

sam two deer walks with a
cane on taos plaza indian
wino with one bad eye
i give him a quarter and
he says it's important
that you get to the origin
of things the origination
all is one one is all
and if you know this
you can figure out the
connections says yeah
i have a weakness cherry
wine is my weakness
says his name is two deer
because he is one of twins
says he can control the
weather give birth to
thunder says white man
black man indian
it makes no difference
we're all the same under
the skin all just as
important as the others
rare to find a brother
like you, though, and i
laugh yeah, i like that
laugh a lot he says come
closer come closer i want
to tell you something
you've got the sign
believe me i know i see
things others do not see
i mean it now you've got
the sign and i see it and
hey you got another quarter?

lightning in slow motion

i am lost in the tracks of midnight
ghost bones drifting in fog
i haunt trainyards and no name hotels
you never feel my arms just my glance
my voice out on the side in the
sweet poison of your agony
if you want to know me you must
go deeper into the mirror and
come out on the other side of silence
where the only battle is the one
with yourself and the only victory
is surrender under a moon of
black cherries we exchange whispers
the stars inviting us to dance
and for the first time we begin
to understand motion on the backstairs
under the moon where coyotes fall
like shooting stars you ask me where
we're going i reply everywhere
you come with the night like a fever
you come with the night like the rain
deep in the flesh deep in the dream
sweet magnolia opening in my skull
or willows swishing for an early grave
you have found the secret of touch
and your silence is like being struck
by lightning in slow motion
take my blood take my sweat take my
words take me back to my lone wolf
way of feeling i stand in the night
air while the shadows shiver
and listen to the whispers of the rain

my veins ablaze with juke joints
roadhouses honky tonks the whistle
of the mystery train my wolf-blood
runs hot i've been to the edge of
madness and back i feel your rhythm
in lowdown backstreets your echo
in the night wind and i howl
as i surrender to the darkness

Poetry Is Dangerous, The Poet Is An Outlaw:
Essays on Poetry and the Art of the Individual

Dancing with the Ghosts of the Dead

Poetry is dangerous. Poetry is dangerous because it is untouchable, unreachable, because it is the mystery that cannot be fathomed. Because it is a phantom that cannot be bought. "What is the most valuable thing in the world?" the Zen student asked. And the Zen master answered, "The head of a dead cat, because you cannot put a price on it." Poetry is one of the few things left that is free. And those things that are free are the most dangerous. Ideas. Love. Independence. You cannot put a price on them. Unless they are wild and free they are destroyed. And if you look around you, you will see a lot of destruction, a lot of violence, a lot of competition for power. Poetry is the enemy of death. Poetry is the secret rhythm of living, breathing vitality. Poetry is everywhere and nowhere. It can only be discovered by the poetic eye, the poetic ear, the poetic feel. It can be found in a blues song. It can be found in a line of dialogue from a movie. It can be found in the inflection of a voice. It can be found in the slightest gesture, a glance, a whisper. It is a ghost reality. Ghost language is the province of the artist. Ghosts talking to ghosts is what poetry is about. And ghost language cannot be taught. Ghost language is something you must teach yourself. Vision is something that must be invented. Poetry is that which is created from the void. Poetry is that which is ripped from the guts when you have nothing left. Poetry is that which is turned to raw nerve from humiliation and despair. Poetry is that which survives the terror of existence through the hunger for more life.

The poet is an outlaw. The poet has nothing but himself, his nerve, his skill, his experience. He has nothing but himself with which to face the world. The poet wants to go beyond the normal boundaries, he wants to experiment, to explore, to stalk the unknown, to smash the boundaries. He wants to challenge every accepted way, every structure held sacred. The poet is concerned with his own way and wants to map out a new road. The poet is an outlaw for vitality. He wants to kill the stale, the imprisoning, the negative, the confining, the boring, the stagnating. He wants

75

to create the alive, the electric, the exciting, the affirming, the experimental, the artistic.

Poetry is dangerous. For poetry says there is another way. It is the way of self-creation. It is the way of self-realization. It is the way of creating your own thoughts, your own actions, your own identity. But people do not want to look at themselves. People do not want to create themselves. Who are we? Isn't this the basic question of existence? And who are we, other than what we create ourselves to be? Who are we, other than the particular kind of life and being of which we are the proponents? Who are we, other than what we will ourselves to be? But most people would rather fit themselves into some predetermined category. Poetry is dangerous because it says let's wipe out all categories, to get down to the essence of what we are. Let's wipe out all categories to get down to our real identity. For what we essentially are is what we create, uniquely and individually, and regardless of whatever other role we play, what we create ourselves to be. And the words, the language, that we use to express our vision, is called poetry.

The poet knows that one line can change your life. Let me take a line from a poem of d.a. levy's: "let this be written on the invisible tombstones: you turned away from your infinite self." A line like that can change your life. And, as if that line weren't enough, d.a. levy goes on: "the greatest mystery to haunt you beyond death was knowing in all the years you had been seen only once, perhaps that was the miracle you had been waiting for: someone who heard the unwritten poems." d.a. levy speaks the ghost language of the poet. d.a. levy is a ghost speaking to other poetic ghosts. And he will be speaking to them through the centuries. For there is no time limit on ghost language. When Zen master Ikkyu was about to die, his disciples asked him where he would go after death. Ikkyu replied, "I won't go anywhere; I'll be right here; but don't ask me anything, I won't answer."

Poetry is dangerous. For poetry says "don't let anyone control your life." Poetry says "don't let anything control your life." Poetry says "nothing is real but your own vision." Poetry says "cut away everything that conflicts with your vision." Poetry says "be grateful to your enemies, for they force you to eliminate them, force you to fall back on yourself and your own vision." Poetry says "be grateful to those who betray you, for they force you back on yourself and your own vision." Poetry says "anyone who truly believes in himself and his ideas and pursues his vision alone can conquer the world." The man alone, with a vision, and the belief in his own powers, is a poet. Nothing stands in his way.

The poem is the overflow of the poet's intensified life experience. The success of the poem is dependent on the tension between the poet's vision and the language the poet uses to express that vision. The poet lives his passion, his obsession. Life is a love affair for the poet. And the success of his poetry is dependent upon the power of his personas, the power of his symbols, the power of his use of language, the power of his ideas, the power of his vision. The most powerful poems are a celebration. The celebration of the fusion of the individual and the universal. The celebration of the discovery of the language that makes the poet's vision come alive. The celebration of the passion and obsession that allow the poet to keep searching, keep stalking his vision, keep exploring ways of creating himself.

The Outlaw Spirit in American Culture

The twentieth century was ushered in by two veins of outlaw thought: the American Transcendentalists' philosophy and poetry and the philosophy and poetry of Friedrich Nietzsche. While revolutionary discoveries were being made in the realms of physics and psychology early in the century, equally important discoveries were being made in the realms of art and literature. And the two figures who anticipated these startling discoveries, who really turned the world of art and literature upside down, were Walt Whitman and Friedrich Nietzsche. The essential components of both men's thoughts were these ideas: The artistic individual is alone. This does not mean that he works in a vacuum. This does not mean that he does not have a knowledge of art and literature. This knowledge is essential. The artistic individual must search and explore and know. Then, he must go into the desert of solitude, unlearn all that he has taught himself, and begin anew, *to create himself.* This does not mean that the artistic individual is particularly anti-social. His everyday life is similar to that of anyone else. But his poetic life, his imaginary life, his creative life is that of outlaw, visionary, and guru. The artistic individual after Whitman and Nietzsche could not call himself poet unless his art involved the risk of challenging everything: art, religion, society, culture, psychology, and arriving at answers which satisfied himself as an individual. It meant exploring the unconscious as well as the conscious; it meant losing himself as well as finding himself; it meant having control over his own life and at the same time being willing to let go, to have the spontaneity of dance. It meant finding a universality in individuality. It meant being an original but connecting with ancient truths at the same time. Nietzsche would go back to Greek culture for the crux of his thought. The American Transcendentalists would go back to Oriental thought for the source of many of their ideas. And, by means of this obsessive journey to universal truths through self-discovery, the artist would yield his work of art. Whitman's *Leaves of Grass* and Nietzsche's *Thus Spake Zarathustra* were two of the first examples of this revolution in art and literature.

Two words hold the key to the revolution of thought spawned by the ideas of Whitman and Nietzsche: energy and integrity. To know oneself, these thinkers said, is to squeeze the essence out of reality, to seek a truth beyond the everyday truth, to become the warrior of a new reality, the renegade of a new integrity. The first observation of the world by these men is that there is nowhere to turn for the answers about existence. There are clues, but no answers. Our predecessors, for the most part, are extremely flawed, extremely primitive, extremely biased, extremely limited. So, the true artist and true thinker must stalk endlessly a variety of ideas, a variety of models, a variety of cultures, a variety of individuals. There is anger and frustration for the true artist and true thinker because there is no way that has been formulated. Most of the essential ideas have to be dug up by the individual himself. They are not taught as part of formal education, or if they are, they are so twisted as to not be recognized. Rare is the teacher who will teach you to deny him and follow yourself. Rare is the teacher who will help you to teach yourself then forget everything you have taught yourself and start from ground zero to create yourself, to formulate your own identity. The artists and thinkers who followed Whitman and Nietzsche wrote and thought with a vengeance, as if to get even for the fact that they had no teachers, no models, no family, no religion, no structure. I am talking about some of the greatest thinkers and artists of the twentieth century: D. H. Lawrence, Henry Miller, Federico Garcia Lorca, Andre Breton, and Jack Kerouac. They thought and wrote with a vengeance: the vengeance of individuality, the vengeance of passion, the vengeance of independence, the vengeance of creativity. They wrote and thought as warriors who were retaliating against a universe that brought them into being with no answers and very few clues. To discover anything required an incredible energy, an obsessive questioning, a stalking of the unknown. Their works of art were almost a retribution to a hostile universe. But they answered hate with love, violence with passion, apathy with a commitment to their own individuality, relentless attacks with an overwhelming positive energy.

The one thing these artists did have, besides themselves, was a sense of place, of locale, a legitimate history of place, if not a history of what it means to be an individual. Federico Garcia Lorca was Spain itself. Andre Breton was a Frenchman as well as an individual. Henry Miller and Jack Kerouac were quintessential Americans. Garcia Lorca used traditional symbols to express a futuristic, surrealistic universe: gypsies, bullfighters, olive trees, flamenco guitarists, deep song. Miller and Kerouac used tremendously evocative American ideas: the open road, the vagabond poet, blues and jazz, the mystery of sensuality, independence at all costs. One cannot touch the best of twentieth-century American writing without reading the essays of Henry Miller or Jack Kerouac's novel, *On the Road*. But they were more than writers, more than literary figures. They were cultural symbols, models for self-development. Their message was: You can accomplish anything, if you believe in yourself. They felt that obstacles were to be overcome, failures to be absorbed as a means to greater strength, defeat to be turned to victory, pain as a prelude to joy, death as a prelude to rebirth. They saw themselves as dancers always in the middle of creating their latest dance, jazzmen always improvising their latest solos, bluesmen always shouting their latest songs.

Henry Miller and Jack Kerouac laid the groundwork for an explosion in the arts around mid-century in America. It was a time for individual artists to single-handedly revolutionize their art forms. In 1955, Miles Davis and John Coltrane wrote and performed an album that changed the history of jazz, an album called *Kind of Blue*. The albums by Miles Davis and John Coltrane and their respective jazz groups that followed this landmark album provide the richest recordings in the history of jazz. Davis and Coltrane continually went beyond themselves in their compositions and improvisations and provided a source of music that compares with any music anywhere and anytime. In the early 1960s, Columbia Records released Robert Johnson's Dallas and San Antonio Vocalion blues sessions, Johnson's only recorded work. These 1930s recordings are the most classic blues recordings ever made, and exhibited the essence of the outlaw spirit: the isolated artist, who, through sheer effort of will, wrote, sang, and played guitar to evoke some of the deepest and most exhilarating moments in the history of the blues. In 1954, Elvis Presley walked into Sam Phillips' Sun studios in Memphis for the infamous Sun Sessions. The real birth of rock 'n' roll took place in these sessions. No one in rock 'n' roll since has matched the rhythm, energy, and power of these legendary sessions. Again, by a personal effort of will, the artist transformed history. And perhaps the most evocative symbol of mid-century America was James Dean. In his short life, James Dean transformed not only movies but American culture. His three movies were important not so much as movies, but as to how they set the stage for his acting, which was pure genius. Outside the movies, he was the artist reacting to a hostile universe, and creating with a vehement passion. His life was an exercise in art. Constantly exploring, constantly creating, constantly going beyond himself, he was one of the century's best examples of the outlaw artist.

In a world as fragmented as twentieth-century America, art serves an essential healing purpose. Art reflects the world as well as suggesting modes of behavior, models of development. The healing purpose of art is most evident when the struggle of the individual to meet his challenges through artistic personas is the main object of the work of art. Struggle and the development that ensues through overcoming obstacles, and the growth that accompanies meeting challenges, provide a catharsis for a world of individuals who are facing challenges of their own. The history of the blues is full of these personas, from Bessie Smith to Robert Johnson to Billie Holiday. Jazzmen Miles Davis and John Coltrane exhibited first and foremost an obsessive religious search through the composing and improvising of their music. They were possessed with going beyond themselves, and their music is tremendously healing because of the individual battles going on in their songs. James Dean was a performer who transferred introversion into extroversion. He was the introvert who through going inside himself—through exploring his own unique identity, in this case, largely through his body, through the evocation of gesture and movement, voice and glance and clothes, the way he moved, his hair, his walk, his talk—created a totally revolutionary art. His sensuality was a quiet, introverted sensuality, yet he was wild, in touch with an animal energy that is ancient. Elvis Presley had a similar animal energy. His performances were full of a raw power and an animal magnetism that made most other artists seem tame. He could make you scream and he could make you cry. He was full of jungle heat and voodoo and magnolia and sultry nights. He took you back to tribal ceremonies. He took you back to voodoo rites. The essence of voodoo is that the body is the crossroads of the earth and the spirit. But Presley brought something new to the ancient ceremonies, and that is the individual. One person, the outlaw artist, was the central element of the rock 'n' roll ceremonies. The tribal was turned into a celebration of the individual.

The outlaw artist is obsessed with his art. John Coltrane was so obsessed with jazz that he slept with his saxophone. Robert Johnson was so possessed with the blues that he compared the blues to a hellhound. James Dean was so obsessed with visual evocation that he studied any interesting facial expression or mannerism and practiced copying it in a mirror. Every day has unlimited poetic possibilities: love, humor, passion, struggle, defeat, coming back from defeat, risk, overcoming, dance, letting go, control, power over self, vulnerability, sharing, celebration. Every day has unlimited poetic possibilities, but it is only the poet who recognizes this. Every day has unlimited poetic possibilities, and the only enemy of the poet is that which hinders, that which restricts, that which tries to kill the passionate, obsessive, relentless poetic spirit.

A Revolution of the Individual

In mid-century America, the decade of the fifties, something
happened in the arts, a new energy emerged, and its most
obvious manifestations were in music and literature. Jazz was
giving birth to the cool. And if Charlie Parker was a gigantic
figure, the figures of Miles Davis and John Coltrane would take
jazz even farther. They stretched jazz to its limits, made it a relig-
ious search of the individual, took the music apart and put it back
together again with the religious fervor of prophets. It was a revo-
lution of the individual. At the same time, rock 'n' roll was
emerging. From the Mississippi Delta blues of Robert Johnson,
the Louisiana-Texas blues of Leadbelly, and the Chicago-based
blues of Muddy Waters and Howlin' Wolf, a new sound was
emerging. Little Richard, Chuck Berry, and Elvis Presley were
the rock 'n' roll prophets. Popular music was to never be the
same. And if popular music had been built on individual hero-
worship in the past, Elvis Presley made his predecessors seem
tame by comparison. No one burst on the popular music scene
quite like Elvis Presley. He single-handedly created a music revo-
lution. He took the extreme sensuality of the blues and pushed the
rhythm to a breakneck speed to create the most frenetic music
ever created, that of rockabilly. But, more than that, his perform-
ances were like the rites of primitive ceremonies, a jungle dance
where the gods were not worshipped, but the individual. It was a
revolution of the individual.

America was a place ripe for this mid-century revolution. For
America, more than any country, values individuality and inde-
pendence. The country was founded on principles revolving
around these two words. And the arts of mid-century America
were going to test the limits of individuality and independence.
Perhaps the single most powerful figure of this artistic revolution
of the fifties was neither a musician nor a writer. He was an actor.
Yet no actor came to acting with quite the orientation of James
Dean. It is rare when the passionate forces of the individual meet
the passionate forces of a generation. James Dean came to acting

with the vision of a poet. Like all the figures in this revolution of the individual, James Dean was self-made, self-created, self-developed. Granted they ran into people who honed their talent, who promoted their genius, but by and large, these figures molded the universe to the will of their vision. James Dean was a farm-boy from Indiana. Shy, sensitive, introverted, his mother had died when he was a child. Passionate and athletic, he had starred on his high school basketball team. And, through the guidance of a drama teacher, he developed an interest in acting. James Dean traveled to UCLA to study acting, and later to the Actor's Studio in New York, to study under Lee Strasberg. What made James Dean different from any actor before? The intensity of his vision. He would take acting to a level never reached before. And, amazingly, with only three movies, because he died in a car accident at the age of twenty-four. Like the other figures in the revolution of the individual, the first force is the persona of the individual artist. James Dean was shy, sensitive, introverted with a powerful urge to transmit the introverted world of the poet to the extraverted world of performance. He was also stubborn and controlling, especially of himself and his world. James Dean, like Elvis Presley, came from small-town, rural America. Their roots were in the earth. James Dean came to Hollywood and he would rock the establishment. Never before had a young genius thumbed his nose at the establishment which had made him a star. His message was: "Take my talent, but don't touch me as an individual. Leave me alone. Let me live my life as I please." He lived and died by this philosopy. But, if he was obsessive about his privacy, he was equally obsessive about his art. He made his face, his hair, his body movements into the single most provocative instrument in the history of the motion picture. He studied the expressions of people around him: their movements, their gestures, their thoughts, and like any great artist, he dug into the essence of human nature, what made people tick, and borrowed, stole, ripped off the genius of others to absorb, create, mold his own persona. And he was relentless. His obsessions took him into the night life of the American soul. Into self-obsession. Into the risks of expressing his own vulnerability. Never has self-confession been demonstrated so thoroughly by an actor. And yet never has more been left unsaid. Like the poet, he spoke with symbols and metaphors and with silence.

The figure who turned literature upside down in the fifties came from a small town: Lowell, Massachusetts. His first novel, *The Town and the City,* was an autobiographical novel that celebrated his early life. His name was Jack Kerouac. In 1946, Jack Kerouac met Neal Cassady, the son of a Denver wino, a madcap adventurer who, like James Dean, had a passion for fast cars and a fast life. Kerouac was never the same and experimental American literature was never the same. Neal Cassady's speech and actions were like a jazz solo and jazz improvisation was used as a literary method. Language was to be created spontaneously, out of the moment, and the rhythms and images of everyday life were to be the major inspirations. Jack Kerouac used this method for his novel, *On the Road,* and changed the course of experimental American writing. He also helped change the course of a whole generation, a generation known by the term the Beat Generation. It was a generation built on the search for self, on the spiritual course of self-discovery, on the revolution of the individual. The crux of this Beat revolution is found in the character of Dean Moriarty (patterned after Neal Cassady) in *On the Road.* Dean Moriarty is the most energetic character in American literature. His zest for life is unmatched. He lives to dance. The dance of holy jam sessions of jazz musicians where he bops and wails and sweats and grunts and howls. The dance of the automobile, the car, the jalopy, the machine that symbolizes the freedom of the road, the new horse of the American West. And he is the first mad driver, mad rider of the American West. He travels everywhere: to New York to hang out with the bohemians, to San Francisco to work for the railroad, to Mexico to visit the brothels, to Denver to walk the ghost sidewalks of Larimer Street, to rural America to view the small-town characters, to big-city America to view the incredibly frenetic energy. Dean Moriarty symbolizes the energy of the fifties: intense, naive, obsessive, innocent, sensual, unswerving, extreme, individualistic. A revolution of the individual.

With the advent of the sixties, jazz continued its remarkable evolution. Elvis continued his remarkable array of hit records and then was drafted into military service. While Elvis was in the service, a new force emerged in American music, one which had its roots in the figures of Woody Guthrie and Hank Williams, the first great songwriter of rock music: Bob Dylan. Like Woody Guthrie and Hank Williams, Bob Dylan began as a poet of the people. He had a folk consciousness that spoke of war and racism and the forces that were affecting the social order in the early sixties. If Kerouac had been the voice of the fifties, Dylan was the voice of the sixties. But because the poet follows himself, Dylan abandoned his stance as folk musician to become rock poet, the more important revolution to him being the revolution of the individual. If Presley had been the extrovertive, performance symbol of this revolution of the individual in music, Dylan became the introvertive, songwriting symbol. Dylan brought a sophistication to songwriting that had not been there before. He brought the rhythms of Beat literature and the images of sur-realism to the music. He spawned a whole new generation of songwriters: Neil Young, Lou Reed, Joni Mitchell, Paul Simon, Kris Kristofferson, Jim Morrison, who changed the direction of popular music in America.

The person who combined the performance aura of Elvis Presley and the songwriting skills of Bob Dylan was the lead singer of the Rolling Stones, Mick Jagger. He inherited the mantle of Elvis as the greatest white bluesman. He also inherited the tribal, ceremonial aspect of Presley's performances. It was one of the greatest symbols of the revolution of the individual: the rock hero as an object of celebration in a ceremony with similarities to tribal rites. Presley and Jagger were the most powerful figures of this event, which combined music and rhythm, words and phras-ing, song and dance, and focused on the genius of the individual performer.

All of the figures in the revolution of the individual, with the exception of James Dean, have their roots in the blues. Presley and Jagger with the phenomenon of the white bluesman and performances with similarities to ancient ceremony. Miles Davis and John Coltrane with their far-ranging jazz experimentation that bordered on a religious search. Jack Kerouac and Neal Cassady, who turned jazz improvisation into a literary method. It is the blues which is America's most original gift to world culture.

The first great figure of the blues was Robert Johnson, a Mississippi Delta bluesman of the thirties. He hung around the great Delta bluesmen as a teenager, then disappeared for a couple of years. When he returned to the Delta, he was outplaying, outwriting, outsinging the legendary Delta bluesmen. Immediately rumors began that he had been involved with voodoo, had somehow, through magic or a deal with dark forces, attained a rare genius. Vocalion Records captured his genius in two recording sessions: one in the Gunter Hotel in San Antonio, and one in Dallas. These sessions are some of the most legendary sessions in the history of American music, culture, and art. With twenty-nine songs Robert Johnson sums up the history of the blues to his time. He also becomes the first poet of the blues. Through his own obsessive solitude, he explores his universe and himself, to create private symbols which become universal symbols: the mojo (the magical love charm), the hellhound (the dark force which follows him), the crossroads (the path that must be chosen), the passway (the body, where the physical and the spiritual intersect), and other provocative symbols. Like James Dean, he died an early and violent death. He was murdered in a Mississippi juke joint in a fight over a woman.

If James Dean was the spiritual force behind the art of the fifties, Robert Johnson was the spiritual force behind the art of the sixties. Although his recordings were made in the thirties, his legend was largely underground, until the blues critics of the sixties unveiled his legend. Like James Dean, his persona was largely introvertive. In performance, he often played with his back to the audience. He was a rambler who traveled alone. He was a poet whose obsessive search for an individual truth resulted in an art that was astonishing: hauntingly beautiful, dark and brooding, with a rhythm that anticipated rock 'n' roll. His was the reflection of the American soul in a violent and energetic time: the struggling with dark forces, the healing of sensuality, the spiritual search for self, the revolution of the individual. His spirit can be seen in such sixties musicians as Jim Morrison, Janis Joplin, and Jimi Hendrix.

The Beats, the pre-Beats, and the near-Beats continued to dominate the literature of the individual in the sixties. Jack Kerouac continued to be the dominant literary figure. Allen Ginsberg was the dominant media figure. Other Beat writers who flourished in the sixties were William Burroughs, Lawrence Ferlinghetti, and Gregory Corso. Pre-Beat writers Henry Miller and Hermann Hesse were significant authors who were widely read in the sixties. Henry Miller's writings were like one huge autobiography, and his emphasis was on the exploration of one's own life, one's own vision. Hermann Hesse was another precursor of the Beats with his emphasis on the individual's search for enlightenment and his novels *Steppenwolf* and *Siddartha* attained a resurgence in the sixties. And near-Beat authors, such as J. D. Salinger and Ken Kesey, were explored for their off-beat characters who were passionately searching for an individual revelation.

In the fifties and sixties, something very unusual happened in the arts. The outlaw spirit of the individual artist became a cultural phenomenon. This outlaw spirit is always evident in art. But it is usually underground, usually does not reach the mass market. With Jack Kerouac's *On the Road,* James Dean's movies, the Sun Records sessions with Elvis Presley, the early albums of Bob Dylan, the outlaw spirit of the artist entered the mass media. These artists would not be denied. They had an intensity of vision, a freshness of spirit, and a daring will to initiate new directions in their particular art forms. It was a revolution of the individual.

Poetry and the Art of the Individual

The twentieth century redefined art. The twentieth century redefined the way of looking at the artist. The twentieth century redefined the way of looking at the individual. The predecessors of this artistic revolution were two nineteenth-century thinkers. They were both tortured individuals who said the way to enlightenment was ecstasy. They both felt that real art was the overflow of intensified life experience. They both felt that their words were only legitimate if they came from the intensity of living life to the fullest. They both felt that previous thinkers had missed one important point: that the individual could make his life a poem. More than that, they felt that life was nothing more than that which was created by each individual. They felt that each individual had unlimited capacities for growth, for development, for creativity, for becoming more. The most important battle, they thought, was the battle with yourself. Constantly challenging yourself, constantly testing yourself, constantly going beyond yourself. They both treated the wounded in wars. And they were both deepened by these experiences. Through suffering, through agony, they saw life as governed by a huge lifeforce, a will to power, a will to self-overcoming, a will to self-creation, a will to self-realization through the obsession for more life, through the hunger for more life. They felt that your life was one of choice, one of unlimited choices, unlimited chances for creation, for creating your own life. They felt that each person was an artist whether that person realized it or not. The only difference between people was the intensity of the creative fire.

One of these men was a philosopher. But unlike any previous philosopher, he was also a poet of passion and music, his philosophy sang and rumbled with a dithyrambic rhythm. According to him, the person alone, with a vision, and the will to create his own life, to create his own destiny, is a poet, and an outlaw. This man was the first great prophet of the nineteenth century. For he had a theory of power. He said life was governed by power. From his observations, there were two dominant drives: the desire for

power and the element of fear. When he came to understand fear
as the feeling of an absence of power, he was left with a single
motivating principle for all human actions: the will to power. His
theory was prophetic in a twentieth century full of changes and
shifts of control. But his theory was not primarily for the external.
His theory was primarily for the internal, for the individual. For
the man with the greatest power is the man who is master of him-
self. But to master oneself is the hardest of all tasks. To transmute
the chaos of life into self-overcoming is to experience the one thing
that requires no justification, that is its own justification: joy. He
who had attained that joy would affirm life and live it however
much pain it contained.

The second of these individuals was a poet, but unlike any
poet before. His language was different. He did not write in tradi-
tional forms. He created a form that was as wide and as expansive
as the new territory he was exploring and he called the form free
verse. He was an American and he was obsessed with the idea of
freedom, of independence. His language would be free. His ideas
would be free. His language would be real. His ideas would be
real. Whoever touched his words would be touching living flesh
and blood. He anticipated the twentieth century and its art by
saying create your own form for your own vision. Let your form
be an extension of yourself. It was one of the founding principles
of twentieth-century art. Let your form be an extension of your
vision and experience. Take to the open road. Explore the uni-
verse endlessly. Seek out comrades, fellow artists, similar spirits.
Get in touch with that rare artistic energy that is everywhere. But
it is only the poet who sees it, who feels it, who breathes it. It is
only the poetic part of us that sees it, that feels it, that breathes it.
He said the poet is that part of us which is created when there is
nothing left. The poet is that part of us which is created when we
have gone too far to turn back. The poet is that part of us which is
created when we get in touch with our own identity. The poet is
that part of us which is created when we have experienced life to
such intensity we begin to know who we really are. But it is risky
business. It is dangerous. Following your own vision is dangerous
because it must come first. It requires that you are willing to give

up everything else. It is total or not at all. To be true to yourself, to be true to your vision, requires you to be a warrior. It is a war of love. It is a war of fresh energy. It is a war of universality. It is a war against death. It is a war against destruction. It is a war against stagnation. But the poet, through revealing himself to himself, reaches a wholeness, a universality.

The two individuals of whom I speak are Friedrich Nietzsche and Walt Whitman. There is no evidence that they knew each other's works, but they defined most intensely the artistic revolution which was to come in the twentieth century. Nietzsche's *Thus Spake Zarathustra* and Whitman's *Leaves of Grass* are the two major works which anticipate twentieth-century art. They combine incredibly revolutionary intellectual ideas with a lyrical, passionate, rhythmical poetry. Nietzsche and Whitman are thinkers who sing, singers who think. And these become traits we demand of twentieth-century artists. They raise the role of the poet to the individual who embarks on a religious search for self-realization, and who, if successful, touches an ecstatic universal energy.

The first two inheritors of the Nietzschian/Whitman spirit are a Spanish poet and an American writer of fiction. The Spanish poet is Federico Garcia Lorca and his best-known poem is titled "Lament for Ignacio Sanchez Mejias," and it is one of the greatest twentieth-century poems. The poem is about the death of a friend who was a bullfighter, a poet in the bullring, an artist with a cape. Lorca combines the ancient theme of Spanish suffering and death with a futuristic, surrealistic language. He goes far into the past and far into the future. It is one of the strongest characteristics of twentieth-century poetry: dealing with ancient archetypes through the use of futuristic language. He begins the poem with a line that is both simple and profound, stark and evocative: "at five in the afternoon." Then he repeats the line: "It was exactly five in the afternoon." Then he uses an amazing repetition: "A boy brought the white sheet at five in the afternoon. A trail of lime already prepared at five in the afternoon. The rest was death, and death alone, at five in the afternoon." He continues with the repetition and the poem builds and builds to an amazing crescendo. Lorca deals with bullfighters and gypsies and flamenco guitars and olive trees and blood and love and death and torture to give us the soul of the Spanish poet. An essay of Lorca's also defines the soul of the poet, an essay called "The Theory and Function of the *Duende*." According to Lorca, the essence of Spanish culture was something that was indefinable, something dark and mysterious, a power and not a behavior, a struggle and not a concept. According to Lorca, it was best defined by an old guitarist master, who said, "The *duende* is not in the throat; the *duende* surges up from the soles of the feet." Which means, according to Lorca, that it is not a matter of ability, but of real live form; of blood; of ancient culture; of creative action. He compares the *duende* with the angel and the muse. "Angel and muse come from without," he says, "the angel gives radiance, the muse gives precepts. On the other hand, the *duende* has to be roused in the very cells of the blood. The real struggle is with the *duende*." Who has the *duende*? Nietzsche. Who has the *duende*? Whitman. What has *duende*? "The magical quality of a poem consists in its being always possessed by the *duende*, so that whoever beholds it is baptized with dark water." What has *duende*? Bullfighting. Because, as Lorca says, "The bull has its orbit, the bullfighter his, and between orbit and orbit there exists a point of danger where lies the apex of the terrible game." Who has the *duende*? Lorca gives the example of a dancing contest in Spain among beautiful women and girls "with waists like water," where a woman of eighty carried off the prize merely by raising her arms, throwing back her head, and stamping her feet on the platform.

The other inheritor of the Nietzschean/Whitman spirit is the American writer of fiction and essay, Henry Miller. No one since Whitman has brought such a fresh, innovative, uniquely American style to the English language. At around the age of thirty-five, Henry Miller went through a personal crisis and decided that from that time forward he would pursue his personal vision, his own destiny through writing and living, living and writing. His first move was to go to Paris, where the literary scene was most active. He lived there with very little money, pursuing the literary life, the visionary life, the life of outlaw and poet. For the rest of his life, and he lived to be a very old man, he was one of the dominant creative spirits in American and world literature. In the later years of his life, he settled in Big Sur, California. Henry Miller was the quintessential twentieth-century American artistic spirit. Stubborn. Independent. Iconoclastic. Naive. Passionate. His basic principle was that if you believed in your vision, believed in yourself, no one and nothing could touch you. If you followed your own destiny obsessively, the power of this obsession would make you invulnerable. He read voraciously, imbibing idea after idea after idea, fleshing out his own personal philosophy, poetry, psychology. In an essay called "Reflections On Writing," he states: "Writing, like life itself, is a voyage of discovery. The adventure is a metaphysical one: it is a way of approaching life indirectly, of acquiring a total rather than partial view of the universe. The writer lives between the upper and lower worlds: he takes the path in order eventually to become that path himself." He continues: "I lived out the social problem by dying: the real problem is not one of getting on with one's neighbor or of contributing to the development of one's country, but of discovering one's destiny, of making a life in accord with the deep-centered rhythm of the cosmos. To be able to use the word cosmos boldly, to use the word soul, to deal in things 'spiritual'—and to shun definitions, alibis, proofs, duties. Paradise is everywhere and every road, if one continues along it far enough, leads to it. One can only go forward by going backward and then sideways and then up and then down. There is no progress: there is perpetual movement, displacement, which is circular, spiral, endless. Every man has his own destiny: the only imperative is to follow it, to accept it, no matter where it leads him."

Art would not be the same in the twentieth century. One could not call himself artist, or poet, without an intense search, an obsessive journey toward self-realization. This journey would take the artist to new locales, to an exploration of previous thinkers, to a search for similar creative spirits, to an art that would combine his experiences and writing abilities to yield a universal truth, a cosmological energy.

The Secret Language of the Individual

Poetry is the most personal of the art forms. Poetry is the most individualistic of the art forms. Poetry is the most intimate of the art forms. Poetry deals with the individual going inside himself. Poetry deals with the individual exploring the inner world. Poetry deals with the individual exploring the inner universe to discover, unveil, reveal his own identity to himself. When the poet gets inside himself, he finds that he has not just one identity, but hundreds of identities. These identities are called his personas. It is the poet's business to create, formulate, mold, enhance, fulfill his identities, his personas. Poetry is the search, through the exploration of various identities, for a totality of being. The poet is, first of all, free. The poet is, first of all, independent. The poet is, first of all, the one who demands that there are no barriers, no walls, no restrictions for the exploration, the journey to find himself. The poet says do not let anything get in the way of the pursuance of yourself. The poet demands that nothing get in the way of the exploration of his inner self, of his poetic identity.

Poetry is the secret language of the individual. If the first realization of the poet is that he is free, the second realization is that this freedom allows for the creation of the wholeness of himself. The second realization is that the poet determines his own destiny. The second realization is that the poet can create himself through fulfilling his own identity. This self-creation, self-realization, self-development is tied crucially to language, to the magical property of words. If the poet can get in touch with the magical property of words, the marvelous properties of language, he can get in touch with the magical and marvelous properties of life itself. Poetry is a visionary path to self-awareness through the mystical qualities of language. The poet pursuing his vision through the magical qualities of language connects with the life-force, the universal and secret energy of the individual. Everyday life is marvelous. Yet it is only the poet who recognizes this. Everyday life is magical. Yet it is only the poet who recognizes this. Everyday life is full of ecstatic energy. Yet it is only the poet who recognizes this.

This definition of the poet and of poetry began with a man who is called the father of American poetry. He was called a genius and a quack. He was called the greatest American poet and a madman. He took a great number of risks. He wanted to create and define a uniquely American poetry. He wanted to break down the barriers of language. He wanted to create a literature that was as free and independent as America itself. He wanted his language to be as lyrical and spiritual as the Bible itself. This man was Walt Whitman. He was a tremendously energetic spirit. He was an ecstatic being. He was a visionary and spiritual being. His poetry was an overflow of his intensified life experience. He felt poetry should live and breathe. He felt poetry should be the lifeblood of the poet himself. His poetry was written to be sung, to be chanted, to be wailed, to be performed. His poetry was a song, a dance, a chant, an ecstatic body of spiritual reality. His poetry was rooted in the individual.

The only absolute requirement of poetry is that it be an expression of your deepest self. Poetry is the expression of the unveiling of your deepest self. It is a revealing of your unconscious as well as your conscious self. The unconscious was not explored with any full intensity in poetry until André Breton and the French surrealists began investigating dream reality, automatic writing, and the combination of words that are usually not associated with one another, finding a surreal reality in seemingly illogic combinations of words. This reality is a dream reality, an unconscious reality, an intuitive reality not fathomed by the analytical mind, the logical mind, the intellect. The surrealists believed that the word is extremely mystical. They believed that if the poet has power over words, the poet has power over life. And, through the magical power of language, the poet transfers a sense of the marvelous, transfers a sense of the enormous intensity of life itself.

The poet believes in himself. The poet is sufficient unto himself. That is why he is called an outlaw, a madman, a saint, a renegade. The poet is in touch with his vision. The poet is in touch with the lifeforce. The poet is in touch with the living, breathing, ecstatic beat of the universe. In *The Cosmological Eye*, Henry Miller writes: "I am not against leaders *per se*. On the contrary, I know how necessary they are. They will be necessary as long as men are insufficient unto themselves. As for myself, I need no leader and no god. I am my own leader and my own god. I make my own bibles. *I believe in myself*—that is my whole credo." The poet has no choice. He is his poetry. He is all-consumed by his poetry. When he denies his poetry, he denies himself. When he denies his vision, he denies himself. Poetry says you are nothing except what you create yourself to be. Poetry says you can create yourself to be anything you want to be, as long as what you create is authentically yourself, is what you totally believe.

Federico Garcia Lorca describes the secret energy of the poet in his essay, "The Theory and Function of the *Duende*." According to Lorca, "The arrival of the *duende* always presupposes a radical change in all the forms as they existed on the old plane. It gives a sense of refreshment unknown until then, together with that quality of the just-opening rose, of the miraculous, which comes and instils an almost religious transport . . . this mysterious power that everyone feels but that no philosopher has explained is in fact the spirit of the earth."

America's *duende* is the blues. The basic theme of the blues is struggle. Struggle and victory, struggle and defeat, coming back from defeat, turning defeat into victory. Living close to the edge in order to transmute pain into an intense joy, suffering into a dance. That's what the blues is all about. The blues, as with the *duende*, is found in the dark sounds that relate to death and suffering. Both transmute pain into rhythm, death into beauty, evil into ecstasy. In a poem called "Cante Jondo for Soul Brother Jack Spicer, His Beloved California & Andalusia of Lorca," Steve Jonas compares the blues and the *duende*: "Yellow wind i've seen you mount the green night thru the spines of moon fleckd trees in the half-light. 'duende' 'duende' & yells of: 'Man, he's got it' & another: 'he's got it' For then this *is* Andaluz province. Spicer sd 'doan yew talk to me about j-azz.' Flamenco came up the Mississippi afta it buried its black roots under a N'Orleans cat house.

'hey momma gimme a taste 'o that fine ty'ass you're swingin &
'yass yass yass' 'n that's tjazz that's duende for they talk of
nothing else save 'duende' 'duende' who's got it who ain't—be it
Manitas de Plata's guitarrista or Picasso's advertisements of the
tribes & folly, as thousands roar: '*Man*, he's got it' 'he's got it' 'i
tell you that cat cooks' 'tellin you like it is' 'got flamenco' (that's a
little shit in your blood)."

Poetry is the living, breathing life force. Poetry is that which
is pulled from your guts when you have nothing left. Poetry is
that which is pulled from your guts when you are backed against a
wall. Poetry is that which is pulled from your guts when all you
have left is your nerve, your blood, your vision. The poet is free.
He knows no boundaries. Free to explore the wholeness. Free to
explore the totality. Free to determine his own destiny. Nothing
matters but going beyond himself. Nothing matters but recreating
himself. Poetry is nothing except that which the poet creates out
of the hunger and desperation for his vision. Poetry is nothing ex-
cept the exploration of his deepest self and the expression of that
deepest self as honestly, as candidly, as evocatively as possible.

ABOUT THE AUTHOR

Tony Moffeit is poet-in-residence at the University of Southern Colorado and director of the Pueblo Poetry Project in Pueblo, Colorado. He was the recipient of a National Endowment for the Arts creative writing fellowship in poetry in 1992. Also, in 1992, he was the recipient of a CoVisions grant from the Colorado Council on the Arts to give performance programs with guitarist Rick Terlep. In 1986, he was the recipient of the Jack Kerouac Award from Cherry Valley Editions for his volume of poetry, *Pueblo Blues*. Both a literary and performance artist, he performs regularly with guitarists and dancers, accompanying himself on conga drum. His collaborations include performances with Robert Bly, Clarissa Pinkola Estes and Lyn Lifshin.

ABOUT THE ARTIST

Bill Gersh, painter, sculptor, performance poet, died in Florida in May, 1994. A resident of the Taos area since 1968, his work has been exhibited in Taos, Santa Fe, Houston, and Dallas. Gersh's performance art was an annual attraction at the Taos Poetry Circus. Also, he toured with the jazz and poetry company, Luminous Animal. A major personage in the art and literary community of Taos, he was especially known for his stewardship of artists and his constant commitment to the flame of creativity.

COLOPHON

This first edition of *Poetry is Dangerous, The Poet is an Outlaw* was published in January, 1995 by Floating Island Publications in an edition of 1000 copies, numbered and signed by the author. Printed and bound by McNaughton and Gunn, Inc. Typeset, designed and produced by Michael Sykes at Archetype West in Point Reyes Station, California. The typeface for the text is Baskerville. All artwork is by Bill Gersh.

This is copy number

862

Tony Moffeit

SELECTED TITLES FROM FLOATING ISLAND PUBLICATIONS

Barn Fires by Peter Wild

Desemboque by Frank Graziano

Sleeping With The Enemy by Christina Zawadiwsky

The Golden Legend by Jeffery Beam

Up My Coast by Joanne Kyger

The Open Water by Frank Stewart

Dazzled by Arthur Sze

Drug Abuse in Marin County by Eugene Lesser

Black Ash, Orange Fire by William Witherup

Flying the Red Eye by Frank Stewart

Point Reyes Poems by Robert Bly

Ordinary Messengers by Michael Hannon

Seminary Poems by Diane di Prima

Park by Cole Swensen

The Raven Wakes Me Up by Stephan Torre

Blue Skies by Robert Fromberg

Ten Poems by Issa, English Versions by Robert Bly

Sheet of Glass by Stefanie Marlis

Cazadero Poems by Susan Kennedey & Mike Tuggle

Winter Channels by James Schevill